The Stranger By the Shore

Another great book of love-wisdom, rebels, liberation and spiritual education
In
Poetry and Prose

From

Chevon

Also by *Chevon*

From *Charles the Good Books*

Reflections and Thoughts   These Days of Our Lives

ISBN: 0951706004   **ISBN:** 0951706012
ISBN: 978-0-951706008   **ISBN:** 978-0951706015

Chevon and Flagstone

Studio Albums
From *Touchstone Records*

I've made it to Broadway   Kingston, Jamaica

Flagstone Reggae   The Star

Solar Flair · Christmas Album

Speak the Words (Poems) · The Spoken Words (Poems)

Dubs, Instrumentals & Symphonies · Music-Poems

The Stranger by the Shore

Chevon

Copyright © 2021 Chevon

10-ISBN: 0-9517060-3-9
13-ISBN: 978-0-9517060-3-9

First Published 2021

By:

Charles the Good Books

All rights reserved. No part of this book may be reproduced or transmitted in any form or by any means, electronic or mechanical, including photocopying, recording or by any information storage and retrieval system, without written permission from the Author, or publisher, except for brief quotation in reviews.

The Stranger by the Shore

Chevon

"The people who come to really help us in our lives don't always come as friends or loves ones. In their own negative and opposite ways some people may contribute just as much as those who contribute their direct love, compassion and support." - Chevon

Charles the Good Books

The Stranger by the Shore

Chevon

A book of Poems and Prose

Cover and back photos of Chevon (in Aruba): *Irwin Lewis*

Charles the Good Books 🌑

As I walk the green fields, under blue skies I also love the palm trees and olive groves. The streams of the mountains please me as much as the sea. This life I am now living that is known to other people as Chevon, is to me an interesting one in interesting times. Like all the others, it will come and go with its on-going experience of movement, change and transformation, as with the life of everyone else. We are all just passing through. Hopefully my work and my love would have helped to make it a wonderful life while it lasted. With feelings of love, respect and equality I share this experience of life and my fate with the poor people of this earth. I refuse all medals, honours and awards that like war-memorial days are really tools of management and control by the ruling imperial psychopaths and the traditional oppressors of the public. Like other seekers with a spiritual education and a concept of the mystery and secrets of time I dance to the beat of a different drum. In our love, compassion and mercy we cherish our happiness, but we know that as happy as we can be, we were also born to suffer. –

Chevon – from a talk at Galway University, Ireland

*****

For Ola

Thank you

Buzz Johnson

And

Desmond (Faada) Johnson

Best wishes to Chris Meredith – Reggae Bass Man

Special thanks to you Bertie and thinking of
Thelma, Patrick and Vivienne, Mr. & Mrs. Austin

The Stranger By the Shore

CHEVON

Chevon does not seek the spotlight, but was an early seeker of knowledge and a spiritual education. Caring and supportive, he was never one who yearned for fame and fortune, or high class. He always considered himself to be just one of the many people of God's creation. He always preferred to let his work speak for itself and that it should benefit our human family. Away from the spotlight he has a great sense of humour and is a warm, kind, friendly, and popular person, and not just with his circle of friends – **Mary Zuma.**

Charles the Good Books

Contents

The Stranger by the Shore 18

Paradise Park 19

Blue is the World 20

Much Too Long 22

Changing Times 23

Then and Now 25

The Way of the Light 28

The Last Rose of Summer 31

So Sad to Know You're Leaving 33

Did She Ask about me 34

Thinking of you 36

A Deeper Shade of Brown 37

Farewell My Lovely 38

I've Made It to Broadway 40

Taft Good-Bye 42

I'm Just Passing Through 43

Maroon Soldier 44

Ten Thousand Dreds 46

Go Tell It on the Mountain 48

Sunlight on the Wall 50

The Star 52

Solar Flair	54
The March of the Saints	56
A Boy and a Girl	59
God Bless America	60
Sad Memories	64
Slippin and Slidin	66
The Glorious Freedom Fighters	68
War on the Border	71
Africa Rise again	73
South Africa (1984)	75
Step-up the African Union	77
I am Santa Claus	77
Christmas in the Heart of Africa	85
Who are They	86
The Lost World of the Mohicans	**Error! Bookmark not defined.**
Leaving the Garden of Eden	90
Excursion to the Providence of God	93

The Stranger by the Shore

Before you made my spiritual recognition
I was just a stranger by the shore
Then struck in a moment of deja vu
You recognized your soulmate, as I did too
We embraced tightly as lost love, once found often do
In a world of constant movement change and transformation
The love of my life, will again share our devotion
We've done it many times before in the past,
You recognized my spirit, and I recognized your voice when you asked
Who is the stranger by the shore?

*****

Paradise Park

When we fell in love so long ago it was in Paradise Park
Holding hands we had gone for a walk and the flame of love was sparked
Oh the angels sang their heavenly songs and magic filled the air
And now I've loved you for so long, so special and so dear for so many years
I was so lonely long ago no one could ever know
But then I found the love of my life, thanks to a walk in Paradise Park
Standing under the willow tree just you and me, kissing in the dark
With the moon shining bright that night in Paradise Park.
Now we've come of age and I've loved you every day
And still will when I'm old and grey
You're a devoted wife and the love of my life.
You say you love me in your heart and soul and it will grow more and more as we grow old
The Magic of that night was like a dream to me,
an enchanting fantasy, as the only sound was a gentle breeze and the falling leaves.
Under the willow tree just you and me kissing in the dark,
and the moon shined so bright on that lovely night in Paradise Park.
In ten thousand years I will never forget that night with my wife in Paradise Park.
Hither and thither - with the love of my life here in Paradise Park.

*****

Blue is the World

The blues from a lost love is blowing my mind
And so there is no peace that I can find
My troubled mind is restless with the pain that I feel
And I can't eat, sleep or know what is real

Now blue is the world, but you can't see what I feel
Or the turbulence shaking my heart that is all so real
And I can't believe that we must be apart
While this storm is blowing wild within my heart

The shattered illusions of love are all gone from dreamland
Yet I'm still playing, dancing and singing with the band
But I can't believe that we must be apart
While this storm is blowing in my heart

Knowing you've found someone new
To do all the lovely things I used to do for you
Yet if you need me with you now you could do it if you choose
But your love is gone and that's too much in this world of blues

I'm sitting now in limbo just trying to understand
How long will it take, and will I ever again be your man
There are some feelings that are gone, and there were some
 that you lacked
So now your love is gone and I just can't get it back

 I've got a strong feeling that I'm hurting now for mercy's sake
Cause anytime you'd want to you'd cause my dear heart to break
I thought you'd be mine for keeps

The Stranger by the Shore

Until I heard you talking in your sleep

It was sad to know you weren't true
And there was nothing I could do
I know we haven't had a word all day
But it's all over and done, there's nothing more to say
Yes, our summer has come and gone and that's how it will stay

So blue is the world, but you can't see what I feel
Nor the turbulence in my heart that is so painful and real
And I still can't believe that we must be apart
While this storm is blowing wild within my heart

So blue is the world and the way that I feel
Very painful and unkind, but oh so real
This storm's blowing in this heart of mine,
Makes blue the world that I find
So as it circles and swirl, blue is the world
Blue is the world

*****

Much Too Long

It's time for me to be moving on for I've been staying here much too long

All my life I've heard of places far and wide, but I don't know what's on the other side

I've never left my home town, as anyone can tell you, I've always been around.

Maybe I wasn't wrong but I've been staying here much too long

Now everything is changing and nothing stays the same but my hometown has seen very slow changes and I can't take all the blame.

This place is getting lonely folks are leaving every day, but it seems no one new has come this old way.

I'm singing this sad song cause I've been staying here much too long

My heart needs to share some loving and my soul would like that thrill

It's no more fun just sitting and watching that steep green hill

The walls are getting cracked, my mood is often blue

On the roof and through the windows the trees are growing too.

God knows tomorrow I'll be pushing on cause, I've been staying here much too long

*****

Changing Times

Life goes on day after day
The time and the customs slip away
But we can't see the changes from day to day
Who will leave and who will follow
Who will sink and who will climb
With the ever changing times

They say every man decides his own destiny
But I swear sometimes it don't seem to be
Like how we dream of things before they come to pass
And the beautiful things that just can't last
Who made the plans and who set the stage
For us to reach this uncertain age
Did you hear the church bell's chimes
Caught up in the changing times

We know for sure that things will change
But sometimes, oh, it seems so strange
In my memories are the times that I love best
To help me relieve the emptiness
Who will rough it through Garvey's time
And set us sail on the black star lines
Oh, why can't we keep the ties that bind
In these ever changing times

Were we born to live and born to die
If so, Lord, I wonder why
Will the time spirit tell us where we are
Traveling on this living earthly star
The Lord will be my shepherd
Goodness and mercy my 'bi-words'

I'll keep the ways of righteousness
Though it's hard sometimes I must confess

I've been here since the beginning of time
And I really won't leave until the end of time
But there are many who have come and gone
And there's not even a trace they were even born
Who will keep a watch along the Nile
For what will come with the changing times
Yes, who will keep the watch along the Rhine
For what will come with the changing times

*****

Then and Now

Traveling and performing all over the world
Man, the things I've seen can make an Afro curl. When I last lived in London it was old Londinium. Scotland was Scotia,
Wales was Cymbry, and Paris was Lutetia, Iran was Persia,
But Adowa was Adowa, in the heart of Ethiopia.
In the Olde Du Vi Gorge, in the city by the lake there was a young king called Janon the Great, yes he was a good king, Janon the Great.
There was a young pharaoh, a good friend of mine, now he's Jesse Jackson – still a friend of mine.
I knew John the Baptist when he was Elijah, a slim teenager who was young and fine.
And I knew him again when he was my school friend, as we stood in line.
My mother Lily was known as the lily of the valley, and was Holy Mary's pretty brown sister.
She said, she was proud of her son, and added "I will always love you when all is said and done." The brave African knight from Timbuktu
Had a beautiful wife called Ola, and yes, pretty Shana, she looked a lot like you.
A wild barbarian from the Teutorburg woods, used to murder and steal his victims' goods.
He one day murdered a Roman and a young Persian too,
But was killed by a Nubian who was passing through
Today they are all at the United Nations working for world peace,
But since then the Nubian was a pirate and the barbarian was a noble Apache, called Cochise.

The Stranger by the Shore

There once lived a dinosaur near the coast of Dover
His remains are now in the history museum for his roving days are over.
Today he is our pet dog and we call him Rover.

The coal that was burned today was once part of a tall tree that died many million years ago. It was killed by a wicked weed in a slow way. And at first I didn't know
That the oil from the well was once a part of the sea creatures that lived and died many million years ago.
Spicy grove and cinnamon trees Africa is home to me,
I remember being a young Afro boy lying with a beautiful Afro girl in a prehistoric world.
We were pledging our love under a bright blue African sky.
Within the wherefore and the why the beautiful spirit of that ancient African girl
Now is the same caring angel within my lovely Japanese wife, for such is life.
There was a time when this busy city was a great and silent forest
And there are some who say that these changes are not all for the best.
Some of the dashing and daring things that I did then, in the past when I was young, made me feel very proud and glad.
But now with increased awareness and insight, when all is said and done, they make me feel sad, for I now know that they were bad.
But then as now I did mean well, as we listen to these and other stories I can tell. *Traveling and performing all over the world man, the things I've seen can make an Afro curl.*

So now I watch my son playing ball with his little friends, and then I wondered what it was like when my grandfather also played with his friends at age ten

I can tell you some more but perhaps a little later, we'll then continue and with improvement, our insight into things will get much better. Traveling and performing all over the world man, the things I've seen can make an Afro curl.

[To be continued…]

*****

The Way of the Light

On a hard day and night you went to bed in sadness and gloom.

Covered with feelings of failure and sadness, bereavement and loss, feeling sad and blue, with the weight and sadness of the whole world filled within your room.

You had a dreadful feeling that all is lost and to face another day is a cost too steep and you weep as you seek refuge in sleep.

Your screaming eyes of the day have now given way. Being defeated by deception and lies, you close with sleep your streaming eyes.

Sleep provides shelter from the chaos and disturbance in your mind, and the feeling that all is falling apart, while trying to find peace from the storm that's blowing wild within your heart.

In a life where so many wishing and hoping and dreams had slipped through the cracks and you could not prevent their fall.

You're feeling it's all over and done, it's done, as it was with the setting sun, so with your pillow to cheek and a door that creaked, you turn to face the wall.

In your hour of need when you could not find a friend, and it's now too late to start all over again. It is true, you lost the case against those who harassed, and falsely accused you. Their lies had brought you shame, for they destroyed your character and ruined your good name.

You traveled a long, turbulent and lonely road that until now you were able to manage the setbacks of your heavy load.

But with the sudden loss of your beloved the heartache is much too hard to take.

Your pent up frustration from abuse, humiliation, and injustice over the years that you could no longer bear, were now let loose in tears.

Being a seeker and believer you are aware of the sixth sense, thanks to your own experience, you were heard to whisper. "Gone now forever, but we'll meet again, and I'll say always, you were my best friend."

The Stranger by the Shore

Having met the 'dweller on the threshold', it was you, and you alone that entered the dark night of the soul.

Oh dear friend of mine, thank God that a light did shine, as from sleep to dream, you moved to where there is no passing of time.

From the dark gloom of your room, in the still of the night, you pierced the veil to experience the mystery, wonder and marvel deep within the light.

In an instant deploy, all your sorrow turned to joy, as you experience a mystic revelation that came as you moved through sleep to dream, and then to vision.

All are in step with the anniversary of season, and your awful disappointments, failures, and setbacks in life were necessary, they were later helpful in life and now you know the reason.

Yes within this great light of love you saw the wherefore and the why, and had a better understanding of it all.

In this holy, lovely and wondrous place of such amazing grace, you now know it could not have happened without the great pain and suffering, and your dreadful fall.

The physical world still waits at the back gate, but within your mystic insight, your pain, and shame can now never be the same within the inescapable hand of fate.

As with those who've had a near death experience and cannot fear dying again, so it is with you who now dream within a dream, experiencing a joyful and moving delight within the heart of the light.

Oh, this light of mercy, wisdom and love is guiding your wonderful night and journey into a new morning light.

The familiar faces of loved ones, and other spirit guides you could see that night, moved in and out of the light. They greet, inform and speak of what's right, and all seemed in some way to say 'let it be, let it be.'

A thousand questions and prayers were answered, within that light of the dark night.

Much stranger than fantasy, this spiritual reality has brought great happiness, joy and ecstasy.

Blessed be the ties that bind and God be praised that this light did shine. You were permitted to see what precious sacred mysteries will unfold, on life's journey, as this brilliant light touched your soul.

For those with a mission, and a purpose it is good to be calm, gentle and kind. It helps with serenity, peace and the removal of anxiety from the mind.

As usual you are deeply moved by human kindness, and the love that motivates bravery that are qualities of the finest.

Within this light also shines your own love, mercy, compassion and sympathy through empathy. This marvelous overnight transformation through this gift of vision, knowledge, insight, and world consciousness was granted by divine permission. Our greatest sorrow must always transfer into our greatest joy For such energy must change but cannot be destroyed The cycle of life does not defect from cause and effect

The great joy in the morning did bring reconciliation between two worlds, the spiritual and the physical. Since then the years are mellow and the old pains no longer feel like the unkind cut of a sharp knife, for you have learned from the examination of your past life.

God only knows how the mystery unfolds throughout the land, but you've come to realize it is all part of the divine universal plan.

We may call the Great, Holy, magnificent and Divine Spirit who is our great creator – God, or by a different name. But this brilliant spiritual light and spark, as well as the dark, are from this eternal flame, and so all is bright and beautiful, glorious and right within the way of the light.

*****

The Last Rose of Summer

I remember the feel of what I'm sure was the last breeze of summer. It brought a thrill of happiness and lots of memories but also a tear at that special time of year. Some fashions and friends have come and gone, the party's over and the fair is moving on.

In this transition, the children have left the schoolyard, the summer is gone and it is autumn from here on.

Yet all along the way the street musicians are sending out vibes and sweet melodies of love.

These inspired creators are channeling and crystalizing celestial waves from above.

And so the birds are flying south, the pretty autumn leaves are falling from the trees, even below my window.

Having produced much tasty honey, their dedicated work has stopped, Oh, sweet trickle pop, the bees are now closing shop.

With hues of rosette, it is still a beautiful sunset, and there hasn't been one like it in 10 billion years. But I am missing you and with such heartaches and pain, I think it's gonna rain.

The other red, white and yellow roses were picked this summer, along with the beautiful daffodils, Sweet Williams (Carnations), lilies, daisies, violets and butter cups looking up, for lovers and poets playing lute and lyre, come Nineveh, come Tyre.

Like my dear grandmother this rose will live again, as bud and newborn, they will bloom in physical form, for beyond the veil of life this is the norm.

The sky is still partly blue and I'm feeling fine, knowing I will be seeing you and your lovely face in another time and another place.

The vibrations of love are deep within my soul thus having me in complete control. And though I'm not alone it keeps me in a dream world of my own.

This last rose of summer that is now fading and dying, once bloomed and blossomed with great beauty and fragrance to tell the truth.
Yes graceful like no other just as it was with Mary Jane my Grandmother in her youth.

As I view with relief this rose that bloomed by the churchyard in naked beauty, and I did not forget the fig leaf.
And as I go on my way, I still feel sad at seeing the 3 drops of blood red petals in the snow last valentine's day.
Throughout the universe all things must be in step with the seasons, oh, yes then as now I really felt that way. For all these things and more I'll say come what may.
It is still there near the church yard, evening is its time for slumber, and I did not pick the last rose of summer. But all things in life must move on, and so regardless of sweet refrain, the wind and the rain, the last rose of summer will be gone.
As I am leaving this lovely place in the sun, I know that my time here is over and done.
I feel it will soon start to rain, and I know I won't be back again.
But I will re-appear with sweet greetings and a warm embrace in another time and another place.
Yes in life, as it is with you and I, sigh or cry, all things must move on, and the last rose of summer will soon be gone.

So Sad to Know You're Leaving

You came around today to say that you are going away
Couldn't believe my ears and the pain, oh I wish you would stay
Oh, I didn't know you were planning to go
But this town isn't the same and the wind's called your name
So sad to know you're leaving, oh I'll miss you

You came here today to say that you are going away
Your band is leaving to play in a land far away where you'll stay
Well it hurts to know you're leaving all day I can't stop grieving
Oh, nothing stays the same and faraway places are calling your name
So sad to know you are leaving take good care for I'll miss you

You were someone I could talk to, a lover and a friend,
And all the fun-times that we shared I thought would never end
But there is nothing in this town for you I guess I know it too
You no longer sing the Blues; good luck has smiled on you
You came by today to say that you're going away
Bright and early oh, yes, tomorrow without any delay
I won't try to hold you I wish you all the best
But oh how I'll miss your kisses and caress

This dump of a town cannot hold you no more
But I know that tonight you'll come knocking on my door
So sad to know you're leaving, I love you my dear and I'll miss you
Because you came round today to say that you're going away.

*****

Did She Ask About Me

So nice of you to come backstage
To talk of life in our hometown
Thank you so very much
Nice to know you like our sound
Home's so many miles away
And like a long forgotten age
You said the church is on the hill
And that the old river is running still
But hey when they came over for tea
Was she happy as can be
Can you remember
Did she ask about me

Meet my guitarist – Paul
He's the one that you hear
Playing away as if to say
He would like this building to fall
You said our folks are doing fine
And that you saw a friend of mine
You are my brother
And one I'm oh so happy to see
But on her way to work
Smiling as can be
Try to remember did she ask about me

Yes the music is alright
You saw what it was like tonight
But I sometimes feel so all alone
Like now we're a million miles from home

The Stranger by the Shore

Is my picture still on her wall
Time for my second curtain call
It's too bad you have to go
Just wish you could stay for the second show
Give my love to everyone
And please give this note to Mom
The old professor how is he
Hey, at her birthday party
I wanna know was she still free
And did she seem far away
In the midst of company
Oh, by the way did she ask about me
Try to remember did she ask about me

*****

Thinking of You

I could be stepping in Shana's party,
And be dancing on the floor,
Or be laughing in the hallway,
Standing just outside the door.
So many things that I could do
But instead I'm in my room – thinking of you.

I could be walking by the seaside,
And wet my feet in the rolling tide.
Could go strolling in the moonlight,
Watch the stars shine so bright.
Even cruise up Primrose Lane,
Or down that mystic avenue,
But I'm locked up in my room – thinking of you

Could be at the rebel concert, hmm hm hmm,
For what it's worth
Go see my friends on the corner,
And have a jam session-rocker.
Watch a good home movie with the band for company,
But honey, hmm, I'm in my room thinking of you.

Don't wanna go to the street fair.
It's a brand new day but I don't care.
I don't want a vacation, no sea and sun, rum and fun.
I'm not saying I'm feeling blue
But I can't stop myself from thinking of you.

*****

A Deeper Shade of Brown

She was a warm and lovely Nubian girl.
With such beauty that seemed to be from another world.
I saw her for the first time when she came through the door.
Yet it seemed I knew her from another time and another place before.
She said she was new in town.
And I was deeply attracted to this beautiful lady of the deepest shade of chocolate brown.

Her hair was black and her teeth they were like pearl.
And her pretty brown eyes take me happily to another world
The lights went dim and the music was a soft smooth sound.
Just then her sensuous beauty seemed to turn into an even darker shade of coffee brown. She was dressed in white in the still of the night.
I asked her to dance and it was a quiet romance.
It felt so right when she held me tight.
She was pure honey in a silken gown
And her silky, smooth skin blessed by the sun, seemed [to turn] an even darker shade of honey brown.

Yes, smelling of roses, perfume and primrose in bloom.
Her enchantment was the strongest vibe in the room.
This was a feeling I'd never felt before.
And it started the moment she walked through the door.
I was touched by her Nubian charm so deep down
And she was of the prettiest shade of Afro brown.

Now the days are bright and sunny and sweet.
Oh, as we walk down Melrose Street.
We are now sitting in the park, away from the heart of the town.
And I'm deeply in love with a Nubian beauty, with a deeper shade of brown.

*****

Farewell My Lovely

You're starring in a new Spike Lee Production
Model, fashion and TV show
I saw your picture in the Jet this morning
Yeah, and that's a lovely way to go

Your clothes are made via Fashion Fair
I guess that is where it's at
And you'd love to hang out with folks like Yasser Arafat
They say you dance like Freda Payne
But talk like Joan Fontaine
And vacation in Malagasy, hey, hey, hey

You were at the Democrats convention
And was a sight to see at the Olympic Games
Your friends come from far and wide and own famous names
Julio Iglesias, the Lady Madonna, Muhammad Ali
Yvonne Shaka Shaka, Mutabaruka, Haa, Haa, ha Haa
You've got your Masters from Harvard
And a gift from the great Mikhail-Mikhail
The once great Gorbachev
Oh, how they love you home in Frisco
And know just who you are
But who can guess who wrote the song
That made you a star

Can you really, really remember?
Without feeling the pain
Do you still wish we could start all over again?

Swing low sweet chariot
Swing sweet and low
Farewell my lovely, that's a lovely way to go

*****

I've Made It to Broadway

If you make it to Broadway
Then you're gonna be a star
But for me, oh, Broadway
Was truly difficult and so far
But I was determined
And I wouldn't give it up
Hmm, I'd struggled hard and strained
And I'd sometimes feel the pain
But when the Good Lord heard my prayer
Hmm, he supplied me with my faith
Now I've made it at last
And I can say – at my own rate

I've made it to Broadway
Though it ain't like it used to be
All the bright lights were gone afar
But the Rebel music played for me
I've made it to Broadway
For now they say I'm a star

It took so many auditions
But I'd passed them so sincere
And when they took me to Broadway
There was some magic in the air
Yet there are some new places
Where superstars now show their faces
Should I try to get there somehow?
No, I'll just sing my song for now

I've made it to Broadway

The Stranger by the Shore

Though it ain't like it used to be
All the bright lights are gone afar
Yet the lovely music played for me
I've made it to Broadway
'Cause now they say I am the star
Made it to Broadway
They said I've made it to Broadway

*****

Taft Good-Bye

At first I did not really like the old school,
It was clean and a bit fancy, but that's just one strict rule.
In the principal's office today I was called,
Where I saw my old painting hanging on the wall.

B sixty three was my old music class,
Where I played my guitar in order to pass.
I also like the quiet of the library's day,
But please don't remind me, cause I'm going away.

The new kids are happy and pleased with their school,
There is even some talk of a new swimming pool.
I'd be just as happy except that I know,
My terms are over and I have to go.

Never thought I'd be feeling this way,
I used to look forward and pray for the day.
Yet, I'm missing my school, so much I could cry,
But there'd be no reply when I said, "Taft, Good-Bye."

*****

I'm Just Passing Through

I know I'm not here to stay
And I know this world is not my home
My spiritual home is not so really far away
You may call it heaven or (you may call it) hell
But to each his own
I cherish all the wonderful people and other lives I knew
Who like me were all just passing through
They may be invisible now, where the past, present and future are not separate
And there is no passing of time, which is fine
And from where the discarnate do reincarnate.

*****

Maroon Soldier (Far From Home)

Cudjoe signed the peace treaty so the war is over and, Maroons can now live in peace to farm, hunt, rest, work and play on their own land, or take time out with a lover.
But for a young folk hero –said he
"The streams of the forest I'll now exchange for the sea"
Something was on his mind I now understand
An adventure was planned.
He made Port Royal his base and the 7 seas he roamed
Living with pirates and sailors and seeing places oh, Maroon Soldier so far from home.
You've seen Buccaneers, Moorish soldiers, Conquistadors and Samurai too.
But the girl who made her mark on you was a sister who came from Timbuktu.
As a mercenary you fought in the south of Spain
But to Port Royal often you would come back again.
You would tell one story after another
And lovely gifts you would bring to your dear mother
But when you had an appointment in the heart of Rome
Maroon soldier you were again gone from home.
When you visited your cousins in Freetown, Sierra Leone
They asked about the folks they left back home
Of Inuit - Eskimos Mic Macs and the mixed Maroons who were born in Nova Scotia
And also the last of the Arawak and other Cimaroons of Old Jamaica.
You've sailed the seven seas with the wind to your back
And your flag was once a pirate's cross,
Oh yes, on velvet black.
But for all your treasure and all your gold

The Stranger by the Shore

You are now growing old.
And you still think of an old love
Though she is a long time gone and is no longer around.
You are not really sure of what went down
But she is now a lonely ghost that haunts in the Tower
of London.
She used to talk of Robin and John from the Shire
of Nottingham.
You explained why the Maroons were victorious,
But oh, said she "they were wonderful and glorious."
Tortuga, Port Royal and Maroon Town was your base
and the seven seas you roamed
Living with pirates and sailors and seeing places,
bold Maroon Soldier, so far from home.
There was a burial at sea for your life is over,
It's now the end of a day for an old sea rover.
Yet in the South Seas Arietta Cereco waits for you
With an aching heart and a child you never knew.
You yearned to know what was on the other side
And your dreams came through long before you died.
But you are buried today all alone, Maroon soldier
so far from home.

*****

Ten Thousand Dreds

In the city of Dred, then thousand Dreds
Went stepping in the house of Dred.
Jah, Rastafari – Dred Natty Congo –
Natty in the house of Dred.
They turned their heads to the mount of Zion
And give ye thanks and praise
Then they lick-up the chalice and passed the pipes
Dubbing in the house of Dred.

Fred Locks, Max Romeo and Big Youth know their roots
U-Roy and I yah Marley was red in the house of Dred
No weak heart was allowed to enter into the house of Dred
Peter Tosh, Bunny Wailer and Ras Michael
Saw the Holy Arc Angel There in the house of Dred.
It was a festival of love and peace,
Unity and Ital feast
The day I saw ten thousand Dreds
Skanking in the house of Dred.

Scotty (Chaka Zulu) and the New Breed, the Inner Circles,
Leroy Sibbles and the Heptones,
Toots and the Maytals, Living Truth,
John Holt, Chevon and Flagstone.
We thrilled the people right down to the bone, yeah
Thumping in the house of Dred
We all lifted our voices in songs of praise
While chucking in the house of Dred

Marcia Griffith, Lorna Bennett, Sharon Black and

Sister Joy (White), told the Beard-man "come on in"
Into the house of Dred
The holy trinity, love and divinity,
Father, Son and the Holy Ghost (Mother).
I saw Garvey and Selassie I (yes, Selassie the first)
Together in the house of Dreadlocks Dred.

(For Sachiko Morito and Tochino Jun)
And
[Dedicated to those mentioned]

*****

Go Tell It on the Mountain

Go tell it on the mountain, over the hill and everywhere
Go tell it on the mountain, to let my people go
Go tell it on the mountain, over the hill and far away
Go tell it on the mountain, to let my people go

Who's that out yonder dressed in blue, let my people go
It's the people who suffer, but God loves them too, let my people go
Who are they out yonder dressed in black, let my people go
It's the slavers and oppressors being beaten back, let my people go

Go tell it on the mountain, over the hill and everywhere
Go tell it on the mountain, to let my people go
Go tell it on the mountain, over the hill and far away
Go tell it on the mountain, to let my people go

I see my beautiful people all dressed in rags, let my people go
They are enslaved Afrocans, oppressed and robbed, let my people go
It will take some time but then they'll rise again, let my people go
They will take some time but we will rise again,
And set my people free

Who are those people dressed in white, let my people go
It's my people marching for their civil rights, oh, let my people go
Who's out yonder dressed in white, set my people free
Civil rights soldiers marching all through the night, to set my people free

Go tell it on the mountain, over the hill and everywhere
Go tell it on the mountain, to let my people go

Go tell it on the mountain, over the hill and far away
Go tell it on the mountain, to let my people go

Christmas time again is almost here, let my people go
Let's spread peace and love throughout the years, let my people go

*****

Sunlight on the Wall

Oh, the sunlight on the wall tells me last night has come and gone and any minute now mother will call, she will call.
Oh I don't know why she loves me so and I guess I'll never ever know
But it hurts to know, I'll leave her very soon, this afternoon.
And ever since daddy died, we've been together side by side,
Except the lovely friends I call my own, we've lived together all alone.
So I wonder how it will feel to say goodbye, hmm hm I'm young and fine but still the time is nigh.

There's some sunlight on the wall is it saying, when I leave something high is gonna fall, will it fall.
Will I miss her precious company and the songs she used to sing to me, will I cry, I won't tell no lie.
Oh sunlight on the wall she'll sigh, cause soon I'm gonna say good bye.
Oh sunlight on the wall she'll sigh, cause soon I'm gonna say good bye.

If you could read my mind you would know
I should have left long ago
Oh, I should have left long ago
Cause it's getting late and I have to go
Oh, it's getting late, oh yes and I must go
Oh I should have caught the morning train long ago
You've seen me down there in the valley long ago
Oh lord I have got a heavy load
So I'm running for my life

Chevon wished he had a wife
Down there in the valley long ago
Oh I'm singing with all my heart
Yes I'm pouring my life out in a song
I should have left this kingdom long ago
Oh lord I'm running 90 miles with my back to the wall

And I'm dancing on the floor, yeah dancing for my life
Oh I say I'm running for my life
Chevon running for life

*****

The Star

The hard ground was my bed last night and a rock-stone was the pillow where I laid my head. I remember seeking a job in the many turn-down places, with other sad members of these twenty first century faces. While others would dance at the Disco Lounge, but I could not relate to all those smoky places where the lost souls congregate.
I'd say seek out books of wisdom and not the senseless paperback novels that were so appealing to some. But now my plane's touched down and there's a mob waiting on the ground, while others are waiting at the Cabana, but I wish I was in the heart of Guyana.

Is this what you came for, to see me on the stage floor?
Some of you come from afar 'cause you say I'm your superstar
Oh, I'm so very grateful for the love you give to me
And I must return it to you in the best way I can see
Oh, for all their lovely tunes, there are so many who have gone to ruin
While some are ready to destroy our world
Should we try to stop them, or crave diamonds and pearls?

So call me a rising star, or say, "Rock it Chev"
But peace and love and unity that's really what I want to give
Wealth or fame can't help me, oh no, not in my hour of need
Or it surely would have saved some from their suicides indeed
Oh, I have no need for special attention
Don't really get excited when my name is mentioned
I don't find true happiness in the fleeting glitter
My true values are down to earth, and so much better

The jet set life don't burn in my soul
They say its hell once you start getting old
When your friends don't come round any more

The Stranger by the Shore

Oft times you're sad and lonely and even wish that you were poor

If we share what we have, for the service of mankind
And model our children from the saints, oh then we'll be doing fine
Instead of pin-up models and useless teenage idols
Show us the world of the prophets
We can't go wrong for choosing it
I'm really just a person, no different from you
Sure I can sing and write a song, try hard, and you can do it too
I don't live for material things, fast cars, furs and rings
These things bring false redemption
In true love lies my salvation

I do the best I can I never worry about competition
I don't run the rat race, I move at a steady pace
I express myself honestly and it sometimes sets me free
Please don't idolize me, I'm not as perfect as can be
If daily I can help someone, or help to save our world from war
Then you can say, in a small way, that I am a shining star
But I'll sing the songs you want to hear and keep my thoughts in my mind
Cause any way you might not care for these words, sound so unkind
I'll sing for you near and far – Oh, wherever you are
And when you like the songs you'll say, Chevon the Flagstone is my-superstar
But there might be someone next to you who'll know you're a star
And that someone next to you will also be a star.

*****

Solar Flair

He's got positive attraction, can do no wrong.
All over the world they love his songs,
And he seems to be in a world of his own
But he's the brightest star you've ever known.
With his radiant smile so warm and clear,
He's got solar flair,
I say solar flair.

All the girls just love him so,
They love to follow wherever he goes.
The old folks think he's the greatest thing,
And the kids they all now dig his swing.
Aah, he's a rocker too, without compromise,
Spell-binding you'll come to realize
His magic is always in the air.
He's got solar flair
Oh yeah, solar flair.

His life is a moving kaleidoscope,
He's always high but he never takes dope.
Don't have to worry about things like cash,
For he's daddy's son and he's quite a flash.
Some may say he's just breezing through life.
But he's very deep, can deal with trouble and strife.
With a love so true you can't compare.
It's his solar flair,
I mean solar flair.

His presence is always so excited,
His eyes have the shine and the glow of lightning.
He was a pied piper in a former time
Who was well known for his poetry and rhymes.
Oh, he's a magnetic focus for the cosmic rays.
He energizes his audience in a spiritual way.
They feel his halo effect and they all can share
His solar flair
The solar flair

*****

The March of the Saints

The saints are marching in, and I can see some of the good people we knew within their number.

Yes in that beautiful dimension just on the other side of life there are some wonderful faces I do remember.

Night and day the wishing, hoping and praying by those who care and are hoping to improve the condition worldwide, have been heard within the light on the other side.

These great numbers of saints are marching while some are chanting as they follow the calling of Jesus into the way of the light.

They can hear some of us praying, yes our calling in the night.

A glorious saintly army of love, mercy and compassion are helping in the need for human redemption.

They are singing and chanting, with prayers of loving thoughts to help ease our pain.

They know of his love and mercy and the painful tears of Jesus crying in the rain,

And in Quo Vadis we see him walking to Jerusalem to be crucified again.

The saints are marching for a new heaven and a new earth for its full worth of a world of love, compassion and mercy. They march for the meek and mild and the love of each and every little child.

The merciful saints are moving on their long march to help bring in a world of love and charity with no more wars, oppression or poverty.

As those Sweet Chariots 'Cumbaya' with all the lovely things that we can acquaint, the love of God is guiding the march of the saints.

The Stranger by the Shore

I can see pretty rainbows; sunshine, blue skies and beautiful colors ever most bright, as the saints are joined by ever more loving souls helping us to move from the dark and into the light.

Those saints who gathered at the beautiful river that flows from the home of God, and the glorious angels faithful as ever have now joined
the march of the saints. Here in this wondrous place, filled with amazing grace,
I reflected on the words of Jesus, asking that we love one another, as one human family of mother, father, sister and brother.
In a world of wars, tricks, graft and gloss, poverty, oppression, exploitation, misery and mass victimization, it seems we are lost.

There are voices crying in the wilderness, trying to do right and yes some are praying all through the night. In a world that's falling apart the marching saints still hold us dear and close within their hearts.
On this blessed day the saints are marching and chanting on their mission of mercy for our redemption and then within this holy sight the time fades away.
The past, present and future were no longer separate and my eyes could see a devoted mother who was a beautiful young lady, dearly holding her baby.
At first I thought it was Jesus and Mary, but soon realized it was my mother and I. It was not Joseph by her side, but my dear father in whom she confides.

The saints are marching for our atonement, and for fairness, equality, truth, morality, sharing, caring, human progress, love and enlightenment.
From their heavenly stage they march for a new way of life in a new age.
I then saw the trial of Jesus, and also felt his sorrow and pain on the day he was so sadly crying in the rain.

As these precious sacred scenes unfold the saints are marching to a heavenly beat of love and mercy, untold joy and even fun.

Thank God that before my insight was over and done, I could see the great solar solidarity within the march of the saints, all happening deep within the spiritual dimensions of the earth, moon and the sun.

*****

A Boy and a Girl

Two children have I had on earth
One a girl, one a boy
Their mother suckled both at birth
They are the light of our lives
And our pride and joy
When they slept in the land of nod
Or when they played in the park
There is no doubt about their spark
They are both the children of God.

*****

God Bless America

The founding fathers were all morally honest, honorable, loving caring and sharing. Yes they said that all men are created equal, and in the same breath

These Masonic sexists, hypocrites, racists and slavers of Afros said "give me liberty or give me death."

These highly respected and overrated slavers and victimizers, made great fortunes from enslaved Africans who for hundreds of years could not earn and save a dime, or leave cash or anything of material value to their loved ones after all that time.

These slavers, posers, hypocrites and fakers denied that Africans (even their wet nurse and sex slaves) were fellow human beings, brothers, sisters and were of God's creation, as they destroyed the First American natives and confined the rest to lives of enforced state terror on barren Reservations.

While their slave trade ruined Africa, they all hoped, prayed and sang that God Bless their America. And all of Europe, especially The Northern Protestants were invited to make their fortune in America.

To the land of the free and the home of the brave, it seemed they all come to look for America. Like a flowing stream they came in search of the American dream.

This dream was created and established for Europeans and as in folklore, they prospered in all areas of material life like never before,

Yes they all come to look for America and to fulfill their dreams in America.

Yet, at the end of formal enslavement, but still under full state oppression, The Afros were denied due State Assistance, and inclusion into the New Nation.

Though disallowed the vote, education and official cooperation, to succeed most Afro Americans did try. But cruel laws, evil policies and brute force were used to prevent their equality, and their fair share of the American pie.

Oh, say can you see – by the dawn's early light that they live in racially enforced poverty, in mostly segregated ghettos, and are police-forced to live with institutional oppression, exclusion, demonization, and this they know.

Systematic lynching, exploitation, routine police terror, brutality and murder, effectively invaded their order. Thus, severe lack of opportunity, injustice and grief is the average experience of Afros in America. Oh, how they hope that their long nightmare will become a sweet dream when God bless their America.

They are still being unreasonably hated, devalued, unappreciated and denied due reward. And after serving the horror of over 400 years of free slave-labor, with no compensation, this ungrateful outcome is very hard.

Forbidden basic opportunities and the great, easy and sweet success as others, some Afros did ask, am I not a man and a brother?

Some do achieve success, usually by stealth and against great odds. And many still believe that their lives, their success and the universe are all due to a Caucasian man that they are told is their only God.

But they and their success are naturally, systematically and institutionally targeted for destruction, tax traps and ruin, while they are hearing the system's sweet jingles, yes those friendly, clever and lovely tunes.

American foreign policy is a successful extension of its domestic policy, it is to racially oppress, exploit and impoverish non-Caucasians.

It creates a world that benefits Euro America and Caucasians of all nations, and especially themselves - the masonic, elite, ruling one per cent.

Being denied the democracy and wealth of most Euro states and as America prevents their democracy, while claiming with hypocrisy to be fighting for their nations, yes; even in Africa they sing God Bless America.

And when this oppressed and impoverished world receive American aid, but not fair trade, they all say God Bless America. From the various lands of their birth people pay homage to the greatest ever racist, covert imperial empire on earth, saying God Bless America.

And so as in New Rochelle, Poughkeepsie, Mineola, Kalamazoo, Saginaw, San Jose, Compton, Sedona, Nogales, El Paso, Reno, Seattle, Oakland, Atlanta, Harlem and in the heart of Santa Barbara, you can see people all searching for America.

Afros and other oppressed groups are all still searching for that well Blessed America. They are dreaming and praying for a better life, as they toil in the sweatshops, farms and factories, the unemployment and welfare lines of a cruel and Godless America.

Regardless of how hard they try, most watch from below, and have to carry on with their lives, as their great hopes and precious dreams all die in America. They feel shut out by the merciless suppression, and their chance for progress prevented at all cost. Yet with love and devotion, and painful emotions most suffer their dream's great loss.

Like their enslavement, they live it out, being suppressed in Urbana
While hoping that God will eventually love and bless all of America
Indeed this will happen when there is a removal of all oppressive laws, policy and practice, and corrections are made to the flaws of 1776. Some laws are removed but it's much the same, the cruel, secret policy and practice, malice and the evil crimes of those in power still remain in the game.

When things are put right and there are fair chances and equal opportunity for all, even the prisoners within the halls of Attica will also say, God Bless America.

When there is an end to institutional racism, institutional sexism, and all imperial state oppression, then the gap between the super-rich, the imperial giant corporations and the very poor will be closed within the nation. When the high walls and barriers of our well respected and beloved traditional oppressors are replaced by human rights, and the ruling imperial psychopaths are neutralized, then they and us will realize that we are civilized.

It is the call that eventually there will be a much better America for one and all.
The glorious Afros and other formerly racially persecuted groups will be there. They will be beaming with joy, justice, unity and equality long before the Twilight's Last Gleaming.
Our Human Family will then know that God truly bless our America. They will all come to look for this new transformed and wonderful America, and will joyfully agree that God bless America. Then we the people will all say God Bless America, Our Home Sweet Home.
Yet as the bees work individually, and also in groups within our ecology to make the honeycomb, I pray - God Bless This Wonderful World and all the other brilliant, marvelous and precious lives that also have the right to call it, and this wonderful world - our home.

*****

Sad Memories

We've lived on Earth for millions of years
We don't know where we're going and where we're from
We don't seem to care
I remember sneaking out of high school with Rosie
We'd go to my house and break all the rules
And also how she cried when she found out that I lied
'Twas not her love I was after
She said I only used her
The music was really new and fresh
But all the time I wasted going after money and the flesh
And all the hearts I broke being wild and carefree
Have now left me with sad memories

Oh, the many times I'd lie, now make we want to sigh
And if I could turn back time, I'd love to see that Daddy of mine
Sad about the way my friend said she was used
Being raped, battered and bruised
Oh, the listening ear I gave her, she said I was like a saint
I try, but Lord knows I ain't
Some think I'm so kind, but sometimes I find
The whole thing leaves me with sad memories

The Jews and Arabs exchanged shots today from afar
In a world that's finished with war
And some Africans are fighting while others are starving and dying
Oh, the losses we've been through from World War One and Two
The bums in the street that we won't help to their feet
It seems this world is a gutter, getting worse, not better
Why can't we see?

The Stranger by the Shore

Will our future one-day be lost in the middle of a sad memory?

I can see the misery of the poor
And their billions of tax dollars going away for weapons in distant shores
And all the time we've lost fighting with those we love
Living like serpents instead of doves
Even last night as you were lying next to me
These things did fill me with sad memories

But now the show is over, it's time to leave the stage
I hate to be a grown-up, sometimes I'm so sad, and sometimes I'm so filled with rage
And when I said, "I love you", you might not think it true
But anyway I really do, yes anyway, I really do, trying to tell you, I really do

*****

Slippin and Slidin

It's been 400 years and we've been doing what we were told
But we are maturing now and we're coming in from the cold
I'm impressed with the changes we've made in recent years
We've suffered shame and wicked beatings, crying a million tears
For the powers that be have kept us down, trying to push us even underground
But now we've heard our master's call, and their writing is on the wall
For they're slippin' and slidin' yeah, and now about to fall
They made fools of us in their movies, kept us out of jobs
Put us on their welfare then tell the world that we are slobs
They kill our leaders and even frame others as cheaters
We can see through these tricks no less, 'cause we've been taught by the best
But I've got a message to give to you, oh yes, one and all
That they are slippin' and slidin' yeah, and now about to fall
That they are slippin' and slidin' yeah, and now about to fall
We are on the move and steady coming through, oh that's plain to see
And the reason I have to speak to you is that something is bothering me
You had us placed under heavy manners and loving you for the smiles you faked
 But now we are singing with joy, oh hallelujah,
Your psychological spells we break, the words of our songs are making sense
Hip-hop hippidy hop is of the past tense
We are one people under a groove, no need to stall
'Cause they're slippin' and slidin' yeah, and now about to fall
They're slippin' and slidin' yeah, and now about to fall
Yes, slippin' and slidin' yeah, and now about to fall

The Stranger by the Shore

We have been the losers in this slick game you call life
Yet we have love to give, you can't scare us with the butcher's knife
Stop all these endless coups; a good government will see us through
Blessed are the peacemakers they shall inherit this earth
Oppressors and evildoers, no they won't come to this concert
A better world is what we all need, in this unity of race, gender, class and creed

We're breaking down the wall; tonight we'll be dancing at the ball
'Cause they're slippin' and slidin' yeah, and now about to fall
Hmm, Slippin' and slidin' yeah, and now about to fall
And now about to fall
And now about to fall

*****

The Glorious Freedom Fighters
(Of the Glorious Revolution)

Toussaint Breda, whose name became the sweet Louverture, knew that he had to train former slaves into the world's best fighting army or they all faced the most terrible retribution. With no back up or support from the Maafa oppressed Afro world the glorious freedom fighters of Haiti stood alone. This was the great showdown between the Euro Napoleon and Toussaint who the French called the Afro Napoleon. The glorious freedom fighters took a life and death stand against the mightiest grand armies of the imperial and oppressive French, English and Spanish and won. Flip or flap nothing can change the fact that in history their great deed is done, it's done.

For over a decade the great battles continued, it seemed that the great struggle and the long war of attrition would never end. But with each successive victory the self-esteem and self-confidence, and the acquired skills and fighting abilities grew with the glorious freedom fighters. They learned from their trusted intelligence team that the Spanish forces in the neighboring Dominican Republic were mobilizing for a surprise attack. So they crossed over the border well before dawn to defeat the Spanish and freed their slaves.

The defeated English, who lost over eighty thousand men, did agree to leave and merge their Afro troops in Haiti, to prevent these veterans returning to Jamaica to spread the dreadful news. Today when we see their strong Citadel we remember not the Alamo, but the glorious freedom fighters whose stories we can now tell. Yes those brave and wonderful Afro men who served their country so very well, not so long ago. The Archives showed that Dessalines put many slavers on trial for the murder, rape, mutilation, torture and other high crimes against enslaved Afrocans. His great and consistent military victories had led the

French public to also confess that of the two Napoleons, this Afro one is also best.

In preparation for revolution, all day Dutty Bookeman had whipped up the Voodoo ceremony. In united harmony, all in attendance called upon the God of the sun, the great African Ancestors and their strong spirit guides to help set their African children free. They knew the first plantation that went up in flames would be the start of the revolution to set Haiti free and to remove their humiliation, terror and shame. Sitting Bull would later organize the Ghost Dance and the Sun Dance, but Bookeman energized the Voodoo Dance, with all those attending calling upon the power of God the great universal creator to help them to defeat their ruthless oppressors who claimed to be Christians. With great expectations the secret stockpile of weapons continued with remodels and repairs so fine from enslaved Afro engineers who were also the best at the time.

So the hand that set the first farm alight had sent the mid-night message that all other plantations would soon be burning that night. Thus many of the cruel slaver - terrorists in their cosy beds, their eyes would no longer open, and yet it was, the end of a dream. They would not live to see tomorrow, and they would not live to see Haiti set free by the glorious freedom fighters in their glorious revolution. Some of the slavers escaped to the ships anchored in the harbour, but as with their neighbors, their way of life and the world as they knew it was over. In the heat of the night and the whole country alight, it was the start of the fight and the African freedom fighters knew it would be like no other night.
This preparation and implementation of the glorious revolution also produced the glorious freedom fighters. With no back up or support from the Afro world, they relied on each other, men, women, boys and
girls. However, many years later, the French were able to seek revenge. In disbelief and denial, the Europeans blamed voodoo, smallpox, the wind and the rain for the defeat of their grand armies by the brave former

enslaved. The Western Caucasian rulers then conspired to covertly disempower, undermine, humiliate and impoverish, like a
broken stick, the world's lone Afro Republic. It was part of a grand design to maintain oppression and to destroy the inspiration provided to the Afro world by the glorious freedom fighters and their glorious revolution.

With the old victorious generation gone came a new chance, as the new ones were out maneuvered through puppet dictators and then forced to pay ($21 billion) to France. The cost was compensation for the French defeat, shame and loss. Enduring the blood, sweat and tears of extreme poverty, the huge extortionate debt was paid within 200 years. This tip and other covert strategies succeeded in transforming one of the world's richest countries into the poorest and most oppressive puppet dictatorship. Gone were the days when the rich and prosperous Afro Republic used its constitution to help inspire, free and empower the Afro world. They had heavily financed the revolution of Simon Bolivar, and some of their best generals, veterans and advisors, ensured his victory in the war to free Central and South America.

The suppression of these historical facts and the long years of poverty caused by the political oppression via puppet dictators are now coming to an end. It is time for restitution so Haitians can heal, revive and have fences mend. The long overdue annual world celebration of Haitian independence will be filled with joy, fun, love and happiness. It is time for the great worldwide Afro celebration of music, songs and dance and for the great poets and historians to tell of the glorious revolution. Yes, let us be inspired by the glorious freedom fighters and their glorious revolution, their glorious revolution. Hmm in this way it's done.
It's done the glorious revolution.

*****

War on the Border

Stop Krigen der rasen ved graensen (stop the war that's now raging on the border).
Freedom fighters are striking targets on South Africa's border.
Growing stronger every day their cry is freedom love and truth.
There's got to be a new order hmmm, "Coute que coute"
(cost what it may).
So spread the word to those now fighting on the border.
Yes spread the word to those now fighting on the border.

"Veni, vidi, vici, (I came, I saw, I conquered)
Are words of emperors, sultans and kings.
So how has that helped us spread peace on earth, good will to men?
Oh, who will change the way we are and show us yet a brighter star?
And stop the war that's now raging on the border
Yeah stop the war that's now raging on the border

Atomic weapons are being built by almost every nation.
Secretly they are racing on with expectations.
"De mal en pis" (from bad to worse) we seem to be.
Bid "Sayonara" (Good bye) "S'il vous plait" (if you please)
Cause they won't be too long waiting on the border.
No, they won't be too long waiting on the border.

Nationalism is the root of war and conquest.
International views will help us see our neighbors at best.
Cause people of the world are really one, after all is said and done
So spread the word to those now fighting on the border.
Oh, spread the word to those now fighting on the border.

Warmongers were making plans, Hmmm, "tout a vous"
(at your service)
While freedom fighters were striking South Africa's northern border.
It's a wonderful world or "n'est ce pa" (isn't it so?)
Cause the 5th horseman I just saw.
While Israel watch the Arabs from across the border.
Please won't you stop the troops from massing on the border?
The future of the world is right now on the border.
Is a total destruction the only solution?

(For Hannah Stensgaard)

*****

Africa Rise Again

There'll be many miles of black star liners, when Africa rise again.
The Ku Klux Klan will disintegrate, and call it a day when Africa rise again.
Our world will know no more starvation, when Africa rise again.
Mixed people will be proud of their African roots, when Africa rise again.
The Apartheid state had to fade away, so Africa could rise again.
We smashed the wicked regime and made it crumble and fall,
Cause Africa must rise again.
Before there can be a world destruction, Africa will rise again.
The wicked have been ruling much too long, so Africa will rise again.
Lifetime dictators will be chased away, so Africa can rise again.
Our fathers, who've lived the dark ages, will look down and smile with pride,
To see their sons and daughters take a stand and Africa rise again.
Martin Luther King Jr. will be a guiding saint, when Africa rise again.
This world will have a new economy, cause Africa will rise again.
The Euro racist juries will stop being so spiteful, when Africa rise again.
Neo-colonialism travel and trade will see a great new light,
This world must have a more righteous system, oh Africa rise again.
Our world will feel an injection of health when Africa rise again.
There'll be no more stupid wars in the region cause, Africa rise again.
Nelson Mandela has started a trend, and Africa will rise again.
Oh, brothers and sisters please help me sing, because they cannot stop our thing,
Oh, we'll do our duty and help things through, cause Africa shall rise again.

You know, we've got something they can never take away and it's the love that burns in our souls, so we the children of the African say, Africa will rise again.

The cradle of man and civilization, Africa rise again.
Democracy is spreading from the south to the north, hmm hm hmm Africa rise again.
Julius Malema is a renaissance man, so Africa will rise again.
No matter what the hypocrites may say, we all know we've got our part to play.
The united states of Africa means, yeah, Africa did rise again.
Jessie Jackson or Farrakhan could tell you, how Africa would rise again.
Marcus Garvey's dream will come true, as Africa rise again.
But there'd never been any doubt in our minds that Africa would rise again.
These are the signs I bring to you, Africa will rise again.
These are the things that must come true, Africa will rise again.

South Africa (1984)

Don't forget who you are
And where you stand in the struggle
Some were saying "dump Mayor Koch"
Some were saying "Run Jesse Run"
That we will be better off when these two things are done
They could see the changes coming with a rising feeling to be free
Put our people first care not the cost to you and me
Stop kidding yourself, get in the groove
Cause yes my people we are on the move
Oh, take down this urgent note
Don't forget to vote

Yes the time is coming getting plain to one and all
That if they don't change their ways
then South Africa will have to fall.
It is a testimony of our awful state
And an embarrassment to the human race
They deny Africans their human rights
God is not with them they are not a holy sight
Our people have to ride the back of the trains
They hold little jobs that offer no gains
They can't strike, protest, or take a stand
And an Afro cop dare not arrest a Caucasian man.
If it takes a nuclear war I say to one and all,
South Africa will have to fall.

Our children are denied a proper education
But they are given setbacks and complications
We are treated with scorn because they say we are "black"
We have our cross plus a heavy sack

The Stranger by the Shore

We must carry a pass or go to jail
Your folks may know but you get no bail
Can't travel abroad, or take a plane or a boat
It's a democracy but you cannot vote
And the racists say we don't give a damn
Because we have a friend in Uncle Sam

I say let's smash all these immoral rules
Cause we are gonna sink this ship of fools
And unite all people in a civilized way
Victory will be ours hip, hip, Hurray.
We'll have to pay a price, oh yes one and all
But cost what it will South Africa will have to fall
If it takes a world destruction
South Africa will have to fall
And if blood must run,
South Africa will have to fall

We are mad and we won't take it any more
South Africa will have to fall
And if it takes a third and fourth nuclear war
South Africa will have to fall
We don't permit racist juries in our jurisdiction
They have a peculiar habit of finding us guilty
And we find them guilty too of racial persecution
And so, South Africa did have to fall
Yes, that Apartheid South Africa had to fall

*****

Step up the African Union

It is time to remove all subnormal cowards, corrupt and mentally enslaved fools from African Affairs
And replace them with patriots who are qualified and strong and have no fear
The problems are many and with a sense of urgency must be resolved
In this great emergency of the people who suffer and know we're all involved
Putin called it a "hopeless graveyard," Trump called it a "shithole"
And it is indeed a terrible tragedy for all to behold
Africans live in mass ignorance and poverty that's plain to understand
Apartheid over privileged remainders and racial offenders still control Africa's wealth, resources and best farmlands. This tragedy has just one solution, step-up the African Union

When the Far Right KKK, police, and other racial persecutors routinely murder Afros often after being summoned by a 'Karen,' They are sending a message of fear and despair that they'd like the Afro World to see, and hear and to accept racial oppression and suppression, while the whole world is staring.
Afros are the vast majority in Brazil but are kept in open prison - slums called Favelas
Chinese racial offenders evict Africans into the streets and immoral Arabs still enslave Africans - Selah
It's not just you and me for this would also not sit right with Tosh, Marley, Dube or Fela
It's time for the Diaspora to work together to unite Africa with a very strong resolution
To meet the needs of all Africans, and bravely and nicely step up the African Union

Migrants are risking their lives to escape from Africa to foreign lands
To face criminalization, detention and humiliation, even so these refugees understand
They'll feel better off than Africans in Africa, so what is the dysfunctional AU's remedial plan
Where is the care, pride, love and respect that these people of African descent are all due
With their streaming eyes, they are told many lies, by those who should step up the AU
African leaders must ensure that the scramble for Africa is for Africans only
So that those who promote African affairs in the African way will all feel comely
The new African leaders must be honest, patriotic, inspired and qualified in Critical Race Theory and the geopolitics of world affairs,
They'll be steeped in racial awareness, race pride, and Afro Lives Matter, yes hear me say it loud and clear
The world domination, management, and control by the Racial Empire of the Euro imperial alliance of racial offenders, and oppressors, led by America will be neutralized with the help of the civilized AU's home base in Africa

The Euro imperial racial empire, led by the USA, must pay compensation and free up all its victimized African heads of state, I'm saying this today
With haste, it is time to take back control of Africa's land and resources and there is no time to waste

Do ensure African resources are for African children, and build thousands more universities and hospitals and greatly improve medical care, and social care. Develop a population that's not just beautiful, but whose African education is second to none, being revitalized, fully developed and civilized.

The only way this can be done is to unite and step up the African Union. The political problems of the African Diaspora cannot be solved by a favorite Rapper, individual, or group the political resolution can only come from a mature, dignified and civilized African Union. Step it up, - step it up - step it up - step up the African Union

A mind is a terrible thing to waste and the Afro World is full of perfect bodies and imperfect minds, so with haste let's develop the beautiful African minds to the highest level for an ideal African Home Base.

Africans don't need charity, only good mental health so as to think with clarity

There are lots of evils to be resolved that can only be done if the AU is involved

They include the Windrush type of atrocities, and declaring the KKK, as a racist, terrorist organization. The brave Black Lives Matter Groups will no longer be seen as lonely, abused and defenseless orphans when there is backup from a stepped-up and progressive Home Base at the African Union.

There is still the outstanding issue of enslavement and colonial reparation, and the Pope must apologize for the false image of God as a Caucasian Man.

Africans are the only people who are servants and slaves to others in their own homeland, and so need respect, equality, human rights and effective remedial plans.

It's not right that Africans should be the poorest people on earth (and crippled by charity dependence) when the world's richest continent is the land of their birth

Yet their leaders are the richest on earth, the worst on earth, last the longest on earth, help to cause the greatest suffering on earth, and oh, how it hurts

The British Commonwealth and the French-controlled Africans must be swiftly replaced with the new international Afro-Commonwealth headed by the president of the African Union.

The African Diaspora will then have good reasons to be very proud of being Africans and to discard their Euro-imposed false label of black. They will give it back and mutually back up and support their home base to be relied on when we step up the African Union.

African affairs will then include foolproof plans to end poverty for proper growth, with integrity, a space program, development, and prosperity.

Thanks to the troubleshooting experts of the much improved and new super African Union; theirs will be world-competitive African minds, highly educated, honest, brilliant, and of full worth

They will match and smash in strength and wisdom, the racial criminals and their covert experts.

It is time for a globally recognized African film festival, music festival, Awards, honors and related ceremonies. The African Union's Medals of Honor must replace those of the Euro imperial racial empire that is designed to racially manipulate, subjugate, ridicule, and dishonor.

With love, not hate let's make this the last generation of the very long reign of the subnormal Right Honorable African heads of state. We now realize that they and their foreign managers, saboteurs, and controllers who want them to remain for life must be neutralized.

Most are disrespected worldwide, but lo and behold, African leaders are indeed the worst in the world. Between the lines, we all now know that the International Criminal Court mainly picks on and prosecutes African leaders. Enough people are able and ready to go, but those sub-standard leaders really don't want to know. But our depowered and long-suffering glorious people will surely know God loves them too when we step up the AU.

No pain, no gain this may not sound nice, but freedom comes at a price. The days when African leaders like the three proverbial monkeys would see no evil, hear no evil, speak no evil, - fear all evil, and take no action when its diaspora is being terrorized will no longer be acceptable as the new AU's reaction.

For about two billion Africans, freedom must come and the time is now. The sacrifice of George Floyd has shown us how, and we'll be well blessed to do the rest.

So let's remove all subnormal fools, cowards, collaborators, and mentally enslaved puppet traitors to those like me and you. And ensure we work to step up the AU, yes, step up the African Union, step up the African Union, step up the African Union.

*****

I am Santa Claus

You children are told that I live in the North Pole, but my hometown is not that cold
You may think I am plump, chubby and round as you sing Santa Claus is coming to town
I will be bringing presents for (little) girls and boys who have been good as well as bad
And all those who are glad and sad, for goodness sake they must all learn from their mistakes
Do you really think I travel the world in just one night dropping off presents in every home They don't all have chimneys and I will not be shot breaking and entering all alone.
Some parents will assist in placing presents under the Christmas trees
They will say it's all from me, and until there is an answer, let it be.

Oh, Lord I am Santa Claus and I'd like to do more than just bring presents of gifts and toys
For a more meaningful life I would like to end homelessness, loneliness and spread more joy
I would feel more fulfilled helping to end bigotry, wars, inequality, oppression and poverty
My merry Christmas will come when equal human rights and justice is common practice
For these things there are ruling psychopaths who would seek to destroy Santa Claus
They profit from exploitation, racism, sexism, hateful religious division and barriers of class

With the help of my children I would like to make the brotherhood of man a reality

I want to end the suffering of all our children and stop their dependence on charity.
I, Santa Claus, would like to keep the children safe from guns, knives and violent crimes
This new way is more beneficial than just to make people happy only at Christmastime.

I want to teach my children that it is better to give than to receive, and how to care and share
They will then benefit from mutual care, and grow up in a new and better world that's fair.
It is the birthday of Jesus that I am helping people to celebrate, and not mine
So think of his truth, his mercy, his wisdom and his love, for these are the ties that bind
He asked us to love one another, and forgive each other's sins, and many had tried
And for that he died, after being flogged, humiliated, tortured and crucified.

I, Santa Claus, I am known for just bringing gifts and toys to little girls and boys
While others at festive times overeat and drink, share cards and presents which is the trend
But I say the lovely souls all suffering neglect, abandonment and homelessness must end
Oh yet, I ask this of you in the name of Jesus, the humble, merciful carpenter from Nazareth

Let's move forward with a brave new inspired vision, so fully alert and no more like sheep
We'll think beyond our petty gifts of creating a better world before we drift off to sleep.
I, your Santa Claus, is now on a world mission, and feeling different this time around
So you'd better watch out that things are not the same the next time I come to town

Christmas in the Heart of Africa

The children are all excited, another Christmas is here
Santa Claus will be a kind African, with good cheers for this year
And we will celebrate and sing as they do in Ipanema,
But there is no Christmas like this Christmas in the heart of Africa

Decorations and lights are all over Christmas Market Street
The lovely houses are all full of joy,
Where all the good people meet
Oh, we will celebrate and sing as they do in Jamaica,
But there is no joy like this Christmas in the heart of Africa

Oh, well a long time ago, hmm, before I met you
In spite of white clouds and clear skies
Those happy Christmas were blue
But now we'll sing and celebrate
As in the warmth of California
For there is no delight like
This Christmas in the heart of Africa

*****

Who are They
(And what are they doing there?)

I've just pulled into the driveway
On this lovely, bright and beautiful day
The white clouds are floating by
In a blue and clear wonderful sky
Inside's joy, laughter fun and happiness I hear
But who are they and what are they doing there

I've been away for oh, so long
But so looking forward to seeing everyone
Do you still love me as we swore it would always be
I'm feeling such joy now that I am here to see
That sound of joy, laughter fun and happiness I can hear
But ho are they and what are they doing there

It is the season of goodwill joy and heavenly love
With good tidings and mercy flowing from above
I will always love you so loyal, honest and true
And sing you some songs of redemption too
Inside is the sound of joy and laughter fun and happiness I can hear
But I wonder who are they and what are they doing there

This old house is full of memories
Flowing nicely through this winter breeze
They recall such happiness
Sadness too and all the rest
In the past when such joy, laughter fun and happiness I would hear

I'd know who they were and what they were doing there

The Stranger by the Shore

As I'm approaching the front door
Years of love within will last for evermore
When I appear there may be new memories to share
And I will know who they are and what they are doing there
Yes, then I'll know who are they and what they are doing there
Who are they and what are they doing there

*****

The Lost World of the Mohicans

There was a time not so long ago when there were no cars, trains, and planes to take us to and fro
There were no skyscrapers, concrete jungle, or the mighty jets that roar with a rumble
The clean air, water and pristine forest was free of pollution in that beautiful world of the Mohicans
The lovely days were sunny and bright and childhood was a fun and games and wonderful delights
The nights were quiet and dark when the moon and stars did not shine bright
As then there were no floodlights, streetlights, or dazzling neon-lights
But some young lovers had to change their plans
In that wonderful but now lost world of the Mohicans

The beautiful majestic mountain, from where rivers run so proudly amongst the clouds facing the sun.
While down below in the beautiful and colorful garden forest, life went on day by day as the time slips away
Then came European boats from across the sea and that bright world changed to agony, and misery
With their firearms, alcohol, Christian bibles and an imperial desire to exploit and enslave
There were wars, conflicts and new diseases that struck like a massive wave
Changes had begun to affect the Iroquois - Chippewa, Mic Macs, Mohawks and Huron,
All their visions, dreams, hopes and plans would disappeared
With the lost world of the Mohicans

The old ties with my good people, the land and the ecology were broken

The Stranger by the Shore

The painful death of so many friends, families and our loved ones remained historically unspoken
Spiritual life gradually faded and disappeared as the forces of the material world manifested
Soon all was lost to the changing times, and the pain of mass disintegration
And the unlucky survivors were forced to start a new migration
Oh, as the children sang, laughed and played, they did not understand
They were leaving the once beautiful, happy and wonderful world of the Mohicans

There was a time not so long ago, when there were no cars, trains, and planes to take us to and fro
There were no skyscrapers, concrete jungle, or the mighty jets that roar with a rumble
The clean air, water and pristine forest was free of pollution in that beautiful world of the Mohicans
The lovely days were sunny and bright and childhood was fun and games and wonderful delights
The nights were quiet and dark when the moon and stars did not shine bright
As then there were no floodlights, streetlights, or dazzling neon-lights.
But some young lovers had to change their plans
In that wonderful but now lost world of the Mohicans
Yes hat world ended and a new one began
From the lost world of the Mohicans

*****

Leaving the Garden of Eden

Childhood was fun and happiness and beautiful games all through the day
There was with the love of God also time for learning, work, rest, laughter and play
It was a period of innocence I once thought would always be that way
I remember the calm clear blue skies and magical rainbows, hoping such bliss would always stay
The brooks, rivers and streams, flowers, fruit trees, singing birds and friendly animals were like a dream in Eden
We walked, held hands, sat and talked and were so in love within that sunny, colorful and beautiful garden

However in life there is always movement, change and transformation
Things were changing slowly but I could not see the reformation
The peace and innocence were not all gone, but there was a gradual buildup of burden
There was anxiety, and stress, pressure and storms now and then in the Garden of Eden
There was still no disobedience, or rebellion but things were changing in the Garden of Eden
It was good while it lasted but then there were new toils, challenges and burdens in Eden

New grown up responsibilities grew, the story is not new and my heart must tell you
The joys of dreamland would be over and I'd take up my burden and toil in the Garden of Eden

Maybe it was not meant to last forever, even as day turned to night in that paradise where I've been

There were already trouble and strife, some bereavement and loss, and still more to come

And come the day when there's nothing left to say, but can't imagine I'd be going away

I will be heading west, hoping for the best, knowing I must leave the Garden of Eden

Filled with precious memories, it is with much sadness that I go, even more than you know

Due to changes in life, it is true that we can't go home again even to the Garden of Eden.

One must face the dark night of the soul and the dweller on the threshold and so once twilight is done night must come

There was an incident in the Garden of Eden, of disobedience, rebellion and those who fell

For a time Adam and Eve were doing quite well until they had a very sad story to tell

It was a terrible tragedy then, when prematurely they had to leave home in the Garden of Eden

It is past the cool of the evening and approaching midnight in the garden of good and evil

It's past the time of snakes, the tree of life, temptation, seduction, original sin and the goals of the devil

The effects of those early actions and woes (in Eden) would eventually lead to Jesus, Judas, Christmas and what future effects to come, God only knows

It is the last day in the Garden, the holy ground has hardened and soon I'll be heading west of Eden

When it's past midnight in the Garden of Eden there will be a new day and no turning back

Tomorrow I will be gone from Eden and can no longer return and that reality will be the fact

The world is round and the longest journey, east of Eden, like the furthest road west of the Garden may, with fate take us back to Eden's Gate

The search will go on for Eden, as we hang on to a paradise that some say is forever lost and gone

For those still searching to find it from their long lost visions, memories and dreams

It's like the search for a long dried up stream, or the invisible being who is most supreme

Yet there can be no disconnect from that eternal love that is all around, and not just above

I was a beautiful child in the Garden of Eden, but as an adult had to put away childish things

I can never go home again due to the changes and transformations that life brings

The calm had passed and then storm and rebellion became a reality in the Garden of Eden. There must now be a reckoning and a new way of life in this new world, for we cannot get back into the beautiful Garden. It will exist in our dreams and in our hearts and minds and on the other side of life. But like this world, we too have grown, and must now live with struggle, trouble, some grief, fun, joy and strife.

*****

Excursion to the Providence of God

We'll go in and out the window, in and out the window,
In and out the window, floating on the winds that blow
Away from this sad world and misery, come wander with me
And so we'll Share our ice cream and candy apples before we go.
Let's get out of this Orphanage that we don't like very much
For there are wonderful worlds just waiting for us to get in touch
The last time we went to California, and that place where you were born
Our travel was a pleasant trip and we arrived in the early morn
Over Chinatown and Old Kentucky Avenue, no one could see us
As we fly
But we had a clear and beautiful view above the late-night quiet sky
We've been to many planets at nights and also during the days
And all across the universe and not just the Milky Way
Yes, we'll be rocking rolling riding and traveling far away,
All the way to Mornington's fantastic - marvelous day
With Winking, Blinking and Nod the candy colored Sandman
Will be coming soon
To sprinkle sleepy stardust and sing us a slumber tune
But we'll be rocking, rolling and riding joyful all the way
Moving into morning-town's lovely bright new day
We'll cross the Moon River that's wider than a mile
To the children's Province of God, and greet them with a smile
We had passed the broken windows of the Old Granville Place
To meet Mr. Bojangles, before the morning sun bless your face
There's such a lot to see in this wonderful land
And-amazing mysteries that we will never understand
After the Yellow Brick Road when we reach the meadow by the park and the pond
We'll be over the Rainbow Bridge and the home of Joanne
So with the other children, as in a row we stand

The Stranger by the Shore

With Dorothy and Toto, he'll come to greet us, the kindly pony man
For on his friendly ponies we'll gallop across the midnight sky
And even meet up with ET depending on how high we fly

For a while we'll forget your wheelchair and the braces on your legs
And other sad Orphans, yes folks with no choice or option but to beg
Or feel the desperation of the enslaved who ran away, Ashanti
Or Yoruba
And lost pets that'll never come home, to those who fret,
Sigh and moan, "Come back Little Sheba"
But children cry, dogs bark and mothers weep for the loss
Of young sons, out in the streets
Like Doreen Lawrence they must live on with their pain
In every heartbeat
Our deep feeling of sorrow and woe no one would know
That day we saw three drops of blood in the snow
It was the time we were lost just off St. Charles all alone
And in desperation had to find our own way home
So let's follow ET all the way out to the furthest star
And bring sunbeams and moonbeams back home in a jar
We could also join the march of the saints in the sky
Another spiritual experience to remember by, and by

We'll visit our magical mystery planet that's so far away
With the month of nights and year of days and September drifts
Right into May
Many tears ago we cast our woes away so with all bad dreams
They can no longer stay
Oh, I'm so thankful that every now and then
We visit such enchanting places to help me be myself again
We'll avoid the mass confusion of the world's grand illusions
But still remain jolly and not join those in praise of folly

The Stranger by the Shore

In our memories are those times that we love the best
They provide hope and inspiration and relieve our emptiness
The adults think our invisible friends live only in imagination
But we know of God's love, hidden dominions, providence,
Dimensions and sweet inspiration
Remember the class of Cooley High and all the fun they had
But also Medgar Evers, Harriet Tubman, Ali Baba and Sinbad
Oh that great Harlem Renaissance of those remarkable Afro Contributor
Such tremendous and magnificent talents of creative and inspired
Communicators
If only we could remain here always like Peter Pan in Neverland
And with Dr. Seuss to hear Harpo's Blues whenever we choose
We'd sing with the willow, gentle as a flower, or a soft refrain
And never grow up to live our lives with more grief, hurt and pain
Well it's almost time to go so let's drive our mini go carts
Those toys were from Santa and we don't need a map or chart
For luck we'll take an old church key with a pocketful of beans
And drive through our secret passage in the closet way down to New Orleans
As we sing, laugh and play sharing our fun and happiness and Precious Memories
They'll blow and flow eternally through all the centuries
We'll just cast our fate to the solar wind and universal breeze
Yes, it's fair to say that we'd rather be anywhere else than here today
But this playground in our minds will help us find our way
Much joy and lovely things our easy riding trip will bring
And from the spiritual providence of God we'll get to Mardi Gras
Nice and early before the spring.

*****

1. Eric Bryson (Community Leader - left), Bernie Grant (Tottenham MP) & Chevon (in London) – *Photo: Rev. Kennedy Bedford*

2. Desmond (Faada) Johnson (left), John Agard & Abdul Malik -(Delano DeCoteau), Poets and Writers (In London) - Photo: *Chevon*

3. Chevon & Mike Phillips (writer) – [London]
Photo: *Frederick Williams*

4. Chevon & Poet – Mutabaruka – (NYC) - Photo: *Maryse Kieffer*

5. John Holt & Chevon – (NYC) – Photo: *Margaret Murphy*

6. Poet- Linton Kwesi Johnson – (London) – Photo: *Chevon*

7. Poets & Actors – Belinda Blanchard & Jean Binta Breeze- (London) – Photo: *Chevon*

8. Activist, Writer & Poet - Elean Thomas – (London) Photo: *Chevon*

9. Chevon & the Flagstone Band (Recording session) White Plains, NY Photo: *Linda Raymond-Gordon*

10. Flagstone -Live at the University of Hertfordshire, England - Photo: *Chris Jackson*

11. Chevon – Photo: *Michael O'Halloran*

12. Chevon – Photo: *Beatrice Griffith*

13. Chevon with friends – artists, poets and musicians
(In Roseau, Dominica) - Photo: *Theodore Green*

14. Poetry Festival (in Reykjavik, Iceland) – Photo: *Chevon*

15. Chevon with school children after a performance in Greenland
Photo: *Parnanguau*

16. Chevon - Jam Session (in Galway Bay, Ireland)
Photo: *Michael O'Halloran*

17. Folk Recital in Lapland - Photo: *Chevon*

18. Children in Greenland - Photo: *Chevon*

19. Asafina on Sunday Morning
In Greenland - Photo: *Chevon*

20. Poetry & Folk music Festival (in Suva, Fiji) – Photo: *Chevon*

The Stranger by the Shore

www.ingramcontent.com/pod-product-compliance
Lightning Source LLC
Chambersburg PA
CBHW041806160426
43202CB00001B/5